BECOMING THE HIGHEST EXAMPLE

The Uniting Leadership Guide
for Everyone Living in the Divided World of Today

Milan Podlipný

Becoming the Highest Example

The Uniting Leadership Guide for Everyone Living in the Divided World of Today

Milan Podlipný

Contains practical examples from business, non-profit and private life environments

Published by Podlipny Consulting, s.r.o.
Nové sady 988/2, 602 00 Brno, Czech Republic
www.podlipny.consulting

For local distributors in the Czech Republic: printed by
Tribun EU, s.r.o., Cejl 892/32, 602 00 Brno, Czech Republic
All other distribution: various print-on-demand print houses

Podlipny Consulting, s.r.o. holds the copyright on all illustrations
Concept of illustrations by Milan Podlipný and Anton Duurer
Graphical design of illustrations by Anton Duurer

ISBN 978-80-908030-2-2 (paperback, color interior "gold edition")
ISBN 978-80-908030-0-8 (paperback, black & white interior)
ISBN 978-80-908030-1-5 (online ; kpf)

DEDICATION

I dedicate this book to my ultimate inspiration, my wise and beautiful wife Anna, as well as to all the teachers I've ever had the honour to encounter. My dedication is also addressed to all people around the globe who strive for self-improvement in order to make and leave our world a better place.

Written on Tuesday, 18th of August 2020

Table of contents

LEADERSHIP PRINCIPLES

About the author

MILAN PODLIPNÝ

**CEO and Co-founder of an international educational
non-profit organization (cspii.org)**

Developer of a universal leadership system suitable for all cultures

• • •

Co-developer of a global expansion system for 200+ national branches

• • •

Leading a global team of 20+ nationalities

VIP Ambassador for CSPII

State Leaders & Politicians
Czech Republic, Austria, Slovakia and Germany

• • •

Academia
Israel, Czech Republic, Austria and Hungary

Public Speaker for CSPII

Has spoken in Iceland, Israel, Bulgaria, Lithuania, Austria,
Germany, Poland, Ukraine, USA, Switzerland and Hungary

• • •

Has spoken at conferences and events,
including at the Czech and German Parliaments

• • •

Media appearances in local and national newspapers

Businessman & Advisor

Working in the financial sector, conducted more than 1000 B2C
and 100 B2B meetings

• • •

Advised on as well as personally led international expansion, business
development, distribution & sales strategy for a variety of companies

• • •

Educated and trained 100+ financial advisors

Milan provides Individual & Group Consultancy Services.
For more information and appointments, go to:
www.Podlipny.info

Foreword

The contents of this book contain universal leadership principles. It is written for everyone, regardless of who you are, where you live, what you do, and what your culture or belief system is. You are the example, knowingly or not, to the people around you. This book will guide you to become the highest example a leader can be, so that all types and kinds of people can benefit from your leadership.

Deciding to be the highest example of a leader will determine the way you live the rest of your life as well as determine how you approach and accept your death. Your highest example of leadership determines how the people you lead live their lives, and how the people they lead live their lives and so on — it is an unending chain. Your decision to follow the principles in this book will change the environment around you for the better, and if you share those principles with others and teach them to do the same, it will make the world a better place for all future generations.

This book is written in a straightforward style for everyone and is based on the commonality between people, as we are all human beings and have similar human traits. Now is the best possible time to consciously focus on what we as humanity have in common; what unites us, instead on what divides us.

Some of the principles in this book are already followed by many without even thinking about or noticing them. However, this book gives you the possibility to teach other people in a systematic way, so that they can follow the principles and pass them on to others and begin a chain of leadership learning.

You can also use this book in the copy/paste mode to set up the internal culture in your company, organization, group and/or team of any kind, for your family and, most importantly, for yourself.

It is my deep wish that this book be a beacon — a uniting, guiding light for all humanity. Do not keep these principles to yourself. Teach others and start a chain of knowledge on how to become the highest example of a leader. Let us accomplish a great and amazing mission.

How to use this book correctly

This book is meant to be read from cover to cover and re-read regularly, so that all the principles are refreshed periodically. The human mind tends to get distracted and we forget many things that we learn. Repetitive reading of this book brings your focus back to the core principles and enables you to keep the highest level of leadership in all situations.

Also, this book is meant to be a practical manual for teaching others how to be the highest-level leader possible. Follow the structure below and pass the knowledge along.

The book is divided into ten chapters. Each chapter represents one essential leadership principle:

I.   **Leaders are the highest example**

II.   **Leaders and the vision are inseparable**

III.   **Leaders should not ask anyone to do what they themselves won't do**

IV.   **Leaders work harder than anyone they lead**

V.   **Leaders must see other people on the highest level possible**

VI.   **Leaders must see themselves on the highest level possible**

VII.   **Leaders must take over responsibility immediately**

VIII.   **Leaders are firm when the cooperation begins**

IX.   **Leaders explain the reasons for their requests**

X.   **Leaders create balance**

Every one of the ten chapters is divided into five subchapters, which cover:

COMMON PRACTICE

- Describes the usual tendencies and approaches of leaders observed in our society.

WHY IS IT IMPORTANT?

- Shows what following the leadership principle will bring.

- Shows what breaching the leadership principle will cause.

HOW TO DO IT

- Gives an extended description and a practical application of the leadership principle.

STEPS TO TAKE

- Summarizes the first three subchapters in clear bullet points.

PRACTICAL EXAMPLES

- Shows real-life experience situations contrasting correct and incorrect reactions through the prism of the highest level of leadership.

- Gives examples from the environments of a) business, b) non-profit and c) private life.

- Gives many personal notes and stories.

- Note: If you are using this book to teach the highest leadership principles to others, this subchapter is the perfect place to share your own practical examples.

Every one of the ten essential leadership principles is condensed into an illustration which expresses its core message. All illustrations are simple, so that you can use them as a reminder for yourself or, more importantly, as a visual tool for teaching others.

I.
Leaders are the highest example

COMMON PRACTICE

A classic statement is that "Leaders lead by their own example" — but what does that really mean? Most people in leading positions are "on & off" leaders. This means that they haven't fully embodied a deep understanding what leadership means. They allow to themselves, especially when they think they are not observed, to breach or not follow some of the leadership principles, rules or promises they made.

Leaders who are aware make a division between their private and working life, based on the level of their different activities, but not based on their attitude or behaviour.

All leaders are constantly under the close observation of people they lead. Leadership standards are set in both on & off times. There is nothing like "leadership time off", "leadership break" or "leadership vacation". Every single breach of leadership principles, especially on the micro level, has a cumulative and exponentially destructive effect within the team.

WHY IS IT IMPORTANT?

Leaders earn respect by being persistent in holding on to the principles of leadership and enforcing them. Every breach of any of the leadership principles is immediately followed by a decrease in respect and trust from team members.

Every leadership principle that is correctly followed and appropriately enforced will set up the common standard of individual and team behaviour. This will create an environment where the group regulates itself and all new people will automatically assume those principles without the need for the leader's interference. This saves a massive amount of time and energy for all.

HOW TO DO IT

Decide that however hard the situation may be, you will never be too lenient with yourself and you will stay aware of being the patient example for others with no exceptions. You are the leader 24 hours a day, 365 days a year. From now on, there is no insignificant verbal or written exchange. Any interaction with other people, even one as short as a chat message, is significant once you decide you will be the highest example of a leader.

Every message you send (or don't send), every word you say (or don't say) and every bit of attention you give (or don't give) creates a new example for others. With every reaction or non-reaction, you are setting up the new standard for the environment you are in. As the highest leader, you are always striving for perfection.

You cannot have what you believe is justified anger or jealousy. With those two feelings, you will always lose. You lose both respect and trust. You must avoid them at any cost. Be happy for the successes of people around you. Make it your inner program that you want people around you to "shine", to show what is best in them. The highest leaders are those ones who recognize the jewels that are peoples' qualities and abilities, not those who think that the jewel is themselves. Also, try your best not to get angry with people who need more patience and explanation. Not feeling angry and not expressing anger does not mean that you will become soft. When necessary, you can raise your voice, strongly express your position, or even end a co-operation. However, internally, you must try to keep calm. People around you will be able to feel your calmness behind your strong outer expressions and stay open to you even in tough times.

It is so important to remember that not saying something when you felt you should will bring you big trouble in the future. Understand that every non-reaction is also considered a reaction. If you see any public breach of leadership principles, your reaction or non-reaction decides what will be the new standard for the people you lead.

If you decide to react, be constantly prepared to initiate and enter into unpleasant situations where you have to patiently explain — often through debate — what was breached, why it is important, and how it should be treated from now on. Do not expect instant support from people you lead as they are in their own leadership training. They do not understand all the leadership principles yet. Therefore, such situations are inevitable. Do not fear them and do not avoid them. It's part of the path towards highest leadership.

STEPS TO TAKE

☐ Make an inner decision that you will never step aside and never breach any of the leadership principles in this book.

☐ Understand that to lead people is the highest level of responsibility and a time-consuming task.

- Always try to be 100% conscious in any kind of interactions with all people, not only with those whom you lead.

- Remember that your every reaction or non-reaction sets the standard for the people you lead.

PRACTICAL EXAMPLES

BUSINESS

EMOTIONAL REACTIONS

Incorrect Approach

I have seen, as well as you all have, many leaders publicly expressing their dissatisfaction with a person, situation, or results. This is often connected with a raised voice, red face, unpleasant feelings, and common silence afterwards. Regardless of how much the leader may be right about their cause, there is never a justification for over-emotional reactions. There may be unacceptable behaviour which needs to be addressed, a situation to be clarified or dissatisfactions to be discussed. However, the way it is done will set the new standard for the behaviour of the whole team. Some leaders may feel that their highly emotional behaviour is justified. It's never justified when this behaviour provokes fear in the people they lead.

Correct Approach

If unacceptable behaviour needs to be addressed, the situation clarified or results discussed, you must keep calm inside while expressing your points. With no exceptions. If you cannot keep calm, move your meeting with others to another time. You can react firmly, powerfully and give objective feedback to the whole team or individual. However, inside, you must be in complete peace. People will immediately listen to what you say, be strengthened by how you say it, and they will feel emotional stability from their leader. Therefore, they will not become defensive and, if they are honest enough, they will help you to find the solution, sometimes in unexpected ways.

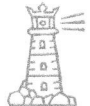

WHEN NO ONE IS LOOKING

Incorrect Approach	I've seen in my life many people who pretended to be leaders, but when they were in their private environment and/or when they thought that no one was looking, they started to speak negatively or with disrespect about their clients or business partners. Many times, I was a witness to such behaviour of high-ranking executives. The consequence of their behaviour is an immediate inner rejection of such a person.
Correct Approach	Leadership is a lifestyle. It is the way to live a life that you can be proud of every single time you look at yourself in the mirror. Everything that you do, write, or say, regardless of whether you are in a private or business environment, imagine that it could be published tomorrow as the headline of the national newspapers. This is how you should consider the way you think, speak, and write about others.

NON-PROFITS

EMOTIONAL REACTIONS | WHEN NO ONE IS LOOKING

Personal Note 	The examples mentioned in for-profit businesses are the same for non-profit organizations. What is different with the non-profits is the missing element of money. Therefore, any breaches of leadership principles are recognizable much sooner in the non-profit environment as people have no monetary reason to silence their dissatisfactions.

EMOTIONAL REACTIONS

Personal Note

To find the best way to prevent negative emotional reactions is up to every leader. First, if you are strong-tempered person, recognize it. Then look around for a method that feels suitable for you to handle your emotions.

One good piece of advice is to include a small time break between working and family time. After you finish your work, do not immediately rush home; take a half hour off for a private routine to "reset" your mind and naturally switch to another role. If you don't do this, then it's probable that you will behave similarly to those close to you as you behave with your co-workers. This micro-break enables a smooth transition between work and personal relationships.

WHEN NO ONE IS LOOKING

Personal Note

Speaking politely and with respect about those close to you, especially in situations when they are not present, is immensely important. There is nothing more hurtful and heartbreaking than when a partner realizes their loved one is speaking about them disrespectfully. Even when your relationship is going through a hard time or ending, don't speak in a negative way about your partner. You do not need to force yourself to speak positively, but the minimum you can do is to maintain "honourable silence". This is valid for all relationships, not only intimate ones.

Of course, it is permissible to share critical, hard facts about someone with others in order to protect both the one you share the facts about and/or those whom you share the facts with. However, you always need to be careful and not "wrap" the shared facts into a net of your own opinions and feelings, which then becomes useless and harmful gossiping.

This is The Highest Example.

II.
Leaders and the vision are inseparable

COMMON PRACTICE

People do not follow a person. People follow the idea the leader represents. Many potentially successful leaders with amazing ideas, regardless of their field of activity, habitually lead and plan in a limited and narrow way. Let's call it "vision-less leading". This approach leads to unwanted and often unexpected results.

Let's look closer at vision-less leading. It's a type of managerial thinking and acting based purely on "bottom-up" planning. Such leaders are aware of their current situation, which they take as the foundation for their future plans. This kind of thinking and planning produces limited results and success. It's like paying the costs for and starting the construction of the house without an idea or visualizing what kind of house we want to build. This is the way that many people lead their businesses, organizations, projects and even their life. In the long-term, it brings the taste of mediocrity. It also discourages others from following the leader.

When the leader does not have a vision, the only thing left for people to observe is the force of the leader's personality, a general good feeling about the provided services or products, and the inner approval of the common plan. However, this is far from a whole-hearted acceptance of a grand vision.

WHY IS IT IMPORTANT?

A leader without a vision — whether it is originally theirs or adopted from someone else — is not a leader. Leading without a vision is not possible. On a day-to-day operative level, it crushes inspiration, creativity, and communication, and the people you lead will have no visionary foundation to help to overcome hard times.

The vision is the main trigger of inspiration for others to follow and for leading them. Regardless of who you are and what you do, your vision will inevitably attract like-minded people wanting to be part of it. They will be attracted and want to join you on your way to help bring the vision to fruition.

HOW TO DO IT

The opposite of the vision-less leading described above is the vision-complete way of leadership. Your future success can be made predictable by

having a precise vision. Here we start to "visualize the house" to see if we like it before we pay for it, plan it, and start laying the bricks.

Most people follow one of the main laws of physics, the classic law of causality, which says that every action has a predictable reaction and corresponding result. We will do it differently, reversing the procedure. It is the same law, but has a different use. Through what I call "reversed causality", every result can be divided into obvious necessary actions so we can create a future that closely resembles our wishes and, in some cases, is even more magnificent and attractive than we ever dreamed. Here is the practical way to do it:

☐ First, you should create a concise **Grand Vision** of the future you wish. Imagine, alone or with your closest partners, a grand future, at a minimum of 30 years from now. Describe how your city, country, continent and world look like after 30 years of your actions. Describe the situation in the present or past tense as if it is happening or has happened. Every Grand Vision should go beyond personal or profit motives and must have a positive impact on the future of mankind. This is what makes any vision a "Grand Vision".

☐ Second, you make an **Extended Grand Vision**. Here, all people you are working or cooperating with are involved. Have them participate and describe the details. The Extended Grand Vision is unchangeable. It will become the Polaris in the night sky, the beacon in the dark for you and all people you lead. A light on which you can always rely.

☐ Third, as soon as the Extended Grand Vision is done, do not plan just yet. Maybe a week later, create the **5-Year Floating Vision** (not a 5-Year Plan — remember! you are visualizing, not yet planning) which should represent the future exactly five years from now. Make sure that your short-term vision fits into your long-term Extended Grand Vision. Adapt your 5-Year Floating Vision every year and invite all people you work or cooperate with to participate. Everyone does this exercise every year. This way, all new people joining you will be able to participate in this process and will feel connected. This will generate a lot of new ideas that you might not come up with yourself.

☐ Fourth, set up the **General Strategy**. The Grand Vision is the final destination, like the ocean at the mouth of the river, while the strategy is like the riverbanks. There are many possible strategies to choose from. The General Strategy does not describe where you are going. It describes by which means you wish the Grand Vision to be achieved. It makes your work focused and straightforward.

☐ Fifth, take the 5-Year Floating Vision and decide what should be the focus in the first year. Then, design a **Short-Term Plan**. This plan is like

the force of the river which will deliver you, step-by-step, to your destination. You can make a 3-Month, 6-Month or 12-Month plan, but not longer. If you wish to learn planning techniques, there are many excellent publications available for your perusal.

☐ Sixth, the Short-Term Plan needs regular **Evaluation & Adaptation**. Regular self- and team-feedback is like the boat service station, where you can refill, patch potential holes, upgrade the engine, or reshuffle the crew.

You, the leader, are here to show the direction through the Grand Vision, the end of the journey (the ocean). The leader helps set up clear boundaries (the riverbanks) through the strategy and guides people down a realistic and practical path through planning (the force of the river). The people you lead are like water in the river, powerful and full of potential, helping to fulfil your Grand Vision.

Finally, I would like to speak about people's inner motivation. I do not use the word "motivation" often, as this is something very personal. Inner motivation can neither be enforced nor created. Whether a person cooperates with you or not is already decided before you say the first word. By sharing the vision, you find out the answer, yes or no. When people speak about "motivating" someone, they mean stimulation.

Here is how inner motivation really works and how it gets unlocked: Your vision is like playing piano or guitar and people's inner motivation is like a tuning fork. When you start to play the song of your vision and it naturally "resonates" with the tuning fork inside of people, there is cooperation. If the vision does not "resonate", you cannot enforce it in any way. Always make sure that you work with people where the sound of the string matches the tuning fork so you won't waste your time or theirs. And don't forget — the vision triggers inner motivation but does not create it.

STEPS TO TAKE

☐ Visualize the far future (a minimum 30 years from now) the way you want it to be.

☐ Visualize the near future (5 years from now) in the way you want it and repeat it every year.

☐ Use the power of "reversed causality" and transfer the vision into a strategy and plan.

☐ Start planning and then put the plan into action.

☐ Evaluate whatever you are doing on a regular basis.

PRACTICAL EXAMPLES

BUSINESS

THE IMPORTANCE OF THE VISION

Incorrect Approach

I have personally worked with and for many companies that had no Grand Vision. To be precise, some had a vision, but only in the company owner's head. It was not written down, expressed or stated for internal company use or externally for the public. When I started to work with them, it was one of the first things I felt it was necessary to correct — to transfer the Grand Vision from the owner's head onto paper. Most of the people who worked for such companies, employed or contracted, were constantly focused on the small steps to be made to beat the competition. For example: to develop a new product, to take an extra percentage point of the market share, etc. The main focus was always on the product or service, not on the "big picture".

This vision-less approach did not keep people in the corporation as it started to grow. The businesses may have initially managed to have little turnover in personnel because of their family environment feeling, but the more they grew, the harder it was to keep employees. This was due to the lack of vision, since over time there is ultimately little difference between the products and services offered on the entire market. One company copies ideas from another. This leads to a turnover of employees where valuable people are lost with the resulting high recruitment and onboarding costs because the company was not able to offer them something more.

A good working environment, enough money and interesting products and services are — from the point of personal development — not enough. People will stay if the leader makes sure that the Grand Vision is adopted by all people in the whole company, and everyone is invited to participate in the whole process described above.

Correct Approach

I have also worked with/for many companies that did have a Grand Vision and the feeling was completely different. People feel an immediate connection if the Grand Vision is something they can identify with. It can provide more inspiration than a bonus, a raise in salary and other benefits. The best thing that companies can do is to offer people participation in the creation of the Extended Vision and/or in the 5-Year Floating Vision, which can be done with even the smallest team. You will immediately see how people blossom and start to find meaning in what they do.

Every employee will see that they are all necessary in the functioning of a healthy, viable company. This is achievable not only through praise and public recognition, but also through offering participation in the vision-making process. This participation is what makes a huge difference. Also, the creation of a vision makes the leadership less personal, since there is a shift from an emphasis on the personality of the leader to an emphasis on the shared vision. This way of functioning will have immediate influence on your success and will be attractive to both co-workers and clients.

NON-PROFITS

THE IMPORTANCE OF THE VISION

Additional Note

In general, the same principles of the vision are valid in the non-profit area, too. There is, however, a slight difference in the non-profits, which are based on non-paid volunteers, without the stimulation of a salary. Therefore, if you work with non-paid volunteers, there is nothing as important as the Grand Vision, as this is the glue to keep everyone working together with you for a long time. The difference between non-profits that survive and those that do not is the greatness of the Grand Vision.

II. Leaders and the vision are inseparable

THE IMPORTANCE OF THE VISION

Incorrect Approach

I've observed many non-profit organizations that have had a short lifespan. They attracted many passionate and active volunteers at first because of what they were doing. However, as time went on, because a vision was missing and also because of how people were led, the organization suffered an extreme level of personnel turnover and then disappeared. Mainly, it was the result of a lack of leadership and organizational structure. Some of the non-paid volunteer organizations were led in a loose manner, which can never result in a full commitment. In others, people were led as participants of a project group with no assigned positions, no structure, and no delegated field of activity. These ways can never result in a feeling of self-owned and accepted responsibility for a task or goal. Neither of these styles fits in the non-profit area as the main way to lead people.

Correct Approach

I successfully lead a global educational non-profit organization with fully non-paid volunteers. The key to its success is what is in this book. For non-profits, there is another extremely important piece of advice: Follow the information in this book precisely. Immediately after joining the organization, give everyone a clear position with an assigned field of activity. Emphasize the responsibility connected with their regular activities and use the leadership tools found in this book as the way to inspire them. Do not treat your recruited people as only external volunteers with no deeper internal involvement. You must make the admission process clear, so that every volunteer you bring onboard shares, knows and identifies with the vision and values that the organization represents.

THE IMPORTANCE OF THE VISION

**Personal
Story**

The importance of a Grand Vision reaches beyond business and non-profit areas, deep into the private lives of all leaders. The personal vision of every leader takes over control over their life. The vision becomes the prism through which decision-making and planning processes are seen. Thanks to the vision, you know where you are going and that every day counts. Your life becomes meaningful.

When I was younger, one of my mentors gave me the task to create an extensive description of "100 life goals", which naturally turned into dreaming how I wished my life to look like in 10, 20, 30, 40, 50 years from then. When I was in the middle of the exercise, all the goals in my mind merged and the vision was created. From that point on, I knew how the rest of my life would look, where I was going and what I would do. I haven't stopped pursuing these goals since.

A few years ago, I interviewed a few happy, older couples who had been together for many years. I asked them what they thought the reason is for their long-lasting and happy relationship. I unanimously got one simple answer - they wanted to live a meaningful life together, and they decided on a common path. To make this idea transferable and practical, let's call it a "couple vision" beyond physical attraction. Creating a common vision for a couple is the next amazing layer of the vision-making process. This shared vision is enormously powerful and keeps the couple together in hard and uneasy times.

This is The Highest Example.

III.
Leaders should not ask anyone to do what they themselves won't do

COMMON PRACTICE

This principle may seem much like principle No. I, which is to be the highest example for others, but it's so significant that it needs its own separate chapter. Many people in leadership positions often ask others to do things they do not do or will not do themselves. When the leader requests others to attend meetings, deliver work on time, be properly dressed, keep all promises made, respond quickly in urgent matters, or keep a certain level of quality in all situations, the leader must adhere to the same demands, with no exceptions. Leaders must not demand from others what they will not do themselves.

Also, this principle is relevant when a team member does not believe that they can do certain things. For example, someone can lack the self-confidence to do an assigned task and/or does not understand why the task is to be done. This is the time for the leader to step in and do it in order to prove it's possible. Most leaders would avoid such an action since it's connected with possible failure or because they feel that it's not their job. However, this is a mistaken view.

WHY IS IT IMPORTANT?

A request to anyone to do something you are not doing or wouldn't do is considered by team members as weakness and sometimes even cowardice or failure. This is not the way leaders should be perceived.

When the leader is prepared to do everything that is asked of others, from that moment on, respect naturally arises. People find it hard to resist any kind of request which is followed by the leader themselves.

HOW TO DO IT

Comply with whatever you teach and request from others. If you excuse yourself once, you are immediately setting up a new standard for others, which will result in ten more excuses from them. A breach of this leadership principle is like a boomerang that will come back to you. It is hard to not deviate from this principle, but it's the only way to earn the respect, understanding, trust, loyalty and support from all the people you lead. You must follow this principle in both cases — when people can see or hear you, and when people cannot.

If there is some occasional unwillingness from the people you lead to do something you've requested, and you've eliminated all possible causes described above, then you have to step in and prove yourself as the leader. You do this by doing it yourself. It might not be necessary to finish the task, but you must start it to show the direction and uncover all the possibilities that people haven't yet seen. However, don't make the mistake of consistently doing the work of others. Do something only if you feel it's a necessary example, and that it will be helpful for the people you lead.

STEPS TO TAKE

☐ Anything that we ask others to do, we have to be able to do ourselves.

☐ If necessary, we must prove to people that it is possible to do more than they think they can.

PRACTICAL EXAMPLES

BUSINESS  | NON-PROFITS

SHOWING THE WAY

Incorrect Approach	I have seen many times that people are lost or question the possibility of doing the work that was assigned to them simply because they haven't seen the "light at the end of the tunnel". I have also seen many leaders who thought they were special and wouldn't do the work that was requested from people they lead. For them, this work was something inferior. The rejection of "showing the way" will ultimately not harm a leader as much as some other breached principles mentioned in this book, but doing it will cause them to gain immense respect from the people they lead.

SHOWING THE WAY

Correct Approach

In the business environment, I've seen many great examples (the best in the Food & Beverage and Hotel businesses) where the top executive joined in with day-to-day business operations when people needed to see how a job should be done properly, or where the manager simply helped in the peak hours. This example is applicable to administration, sales and, of course, to non-profits, too. When people don't understand or doubt themselves, you can always evaluate the situation and jump in to show them what you mean and what you are requesting. Your action opens up the attitude of the people you lead and you immediately earn their respect.

INTIMATE BEHAVIOUR

Incorrect Approach

I have met people in leading positions who had short-term romantic relationships with the people they led. This is completely unacceptable. People notice this behaviour and talk about it. There is an extremely high cost — an immediate loss of respect due to the misuse of the leadership position. I've witnessed many great teams go down because of the lack of self-control of their leaders. This type of behaviour destroys interpersonal relationships in the whole team quickly.

Correct Approach

It is always up to the leader to behave in a way that makes things clear for all. A successful leader should be inspiring, but not create any kind of expectations of a romantic relationship from people they lead.

When there is an intention is to build up a long-term relationship with a team member, then proceed with honesty with the group. However, be very careful that the relationship does not influence your work. Always set up the best possible example for others.

III. Leaders should not ask anyone to do what they themselves won't do

THE ART OF APPRECIATION

Incorrect Approach

Leaders in the non-profit environment can take people's involvement for granted, since many of them come from the business environment. They are used to the idea that appreciation and thankfulness are compensated with a salary, commission, or margin. As this is the basic program in the mind of the business leader, thankfulness and gratitude are usually not expressed enough. However, it is a mistake to think that appreciation and thankfulness are not necessary in any type of business. It is true that it may be not openly requested by people you lead, but it is definitely missed when not expressed enough.

Correct Approach

Appreciation and thankfulness are crucial in both the for-profit and the non-profit area. If you wish to create a working environment where people appreciate each other's work, first you must set the example yourself.

In typical NGOs, people are volunteers and either not paid or paid below the for-profit standard. In such cases, the inner motivation of the workers must be immense and appreciation from the leader constant. You must learn how to thank people properly. A very specific "thank you" expressed orally or in written form for a very specific job done is necessary to make people feel appreciated. Thank people constantly, but always with attention to detail, so that it's obvious you really see their input and mean it honestly. A general "thank you" may be perceived as artificial and superficial. Use a heartfelt "thank you" in both non-profit and for-profit environments.

APPOINTMENT PUNCTUALITY

Incorrect Approach

I have observed during my working life that many owners of companies, directors and managers have the belief that because of their position in the company, coming late to the meetings or not appearing at all does not matter. They believe that they can demand something from their employees because they are paid to follow requests. However, the team members know this is a double standard. This causes a dissatisfaction which they can't or don't express because of fear of losing their job and/or creating some potentially unpleasant working environment with their superior. Therefore, many leaders may think that nothing is wrong, but be sure that around the coffee machine, everyone is expressing their feelings with each other and it's not praise of the executive.

Correct Approach

If the company is leadership-based, there is no excuse for coming a single minute late (or not coming at all) to a meeting with anyone, except for in emergency or life-threatening situations and other such cases. Structurally, there are the leaders and the people who are being led. However, on the level of obeying leadership principles, there is no difference between the positions. Once the leader follows the leadership principles, they can enforce them with dignity and not through threats. This is leading by the highest example. A friend told me once: "If you can, you have to!" Therefore, if you can, always do it. Show people that you see them as equal members of the team and as highly valuable. Show your appreciation through your attitude.

III. Leaders should not ask anyone to do what they themselves won't do

APPOINTMENT PUNCTUALITY

Incorrect Approach

The non-profit environment is the same situation as the for-profit business. Out of pride or lack of understanding, people in leadership positions tend to find their own small excuses for why they don't have to attend a meeting. I've heard a number of reasons including vacation, bank holiday, birthday, sickness, different time zone, etc. Especially in the volunteer non-profits, this approach leads immediately to the setting up of a new standard for the whole team.

Once you, the leader, make any of these excuses, you will receive a thunderstorm of similar ones from others. You must understand that there are millions of reasons for not attending meetings. In the non-profits, it's essential to have fixed regular weekly meetings and have obligatory attendance with the goal of 52 times a year. If you make one exception for someone, when the team is not yet mature enough, or for yourself, from that point on, you have to grant it to all. This is the way to a slow death for your organization. You must be the strictest on yourself before you can request your team members follow these rules.

Correct Approach

I remember a situation when I joined my team meetings online from the hospital, just before a surgery. I had meetings (happening in the Central European Time Zone) in the middle of the night from the Far East of Russia, late night from New Zealand and in the very early morning from the USA. Every such situation is observed by the people you lead. Through your own example, you set up what is an exceptional situation and what is not. So far, I know of nothing that would make me miss a meeting with my team. Literally nothing. Our organization has a noble cause, and I know my responsibility. I also understand all the possible consequences of every single non-attended meeting for the whole team, its integrity and functionality. The bigger the team is, the more excuses will appear, and the stricter you must be on following the rules. It is these rules that hold the team together as a group which works toward the common vision and nothing has higher priority.

ART OF APPRECIATION | APPOINTMENT PUNCTUALITY

**Personal
Story**

In your private life, being punctual for appointments is perceived as appreciation and respect for those you meet with. Friends, family members and life partners are, for the most part, not a business relationship. However, from the perspective of the highest leadership, your family member, husband or wife, child, friend or parent are of no lesser importance than your business colleagues or non-profit team members. If someone in your personal life sees you are always on time in your working life and always late when it comes to them, it does not make them feel good. Therefore, maintain this rule not only in your work, but also in your private life.

The next important point is the expression of thankfulness and appreciation towards your closest ones. The more you focus on the details when you express thankfulness and appreciation, the stronger it is perceived. A "thank you" to your life partner is always a good idea. However, attention to detail really gives weight to your thanks. It is immediately clear that you notice even the smallest things your close one said or did. Expressing thankfulness in such a form is heart-warming, reassuring, and it strengthens your bonds.

This is The Highest Example.

IV.
Leaders work harder than anyone they lead

COMMON PRACTICE

One extreme is that some leaders and/or their team members think that working harder means to work longer. From a leadership perspective, that is not correct, and it is a bad example, regardless of whether it is done by the members or the leader of the team. Every single action or non-action of the leader creates the example for others, good or bad. Downtime and how it is spent also shows an example to others. Many team members and their leaders often have the feeling that the longer they work, the more they will achieve. In their minds, the length of time spent on an activity equals effectiveness and productivity. This approach does not produce long-term happiness and fulfilment for team members, and can lead to heavy burnout.

Another extreme is that leaders delegate so much to others that they don't have tasks left to do themselves. Delegating the workload is sensible and must happen. However, the leader must keep their own non-delegated activities.

Over-delegation of responsibilities by the leader can result in harm to the both the leader and the group. If the leaders stop doing the activities that inspired them and made them feel good, they lose their connection with people, with day-to-day operations, and with their good feelings about themselves.

Another problem is when team members stop dedicating enough time to their activities, and the people they work with recognize that something is not ok. Other team members might start to copy this approach and also work less.

The answer is the balance between these two extremes. Keeping the balance is the constant operative work of the leader — to observe, evaluate and fix, if necessary.

WHY IS IT IMPORTANT?

Working too much creates the risk of burnout for you and your team. If any person in the team works to exhaustion, people start to adapt to this pattern and many can have the feeling that they are not doing enough. On the other hand, working too little creates the risk of everyone of losing effectiveness, productivity and especially inspiration. Because every leader must produce some results, delivering the proper results may be endangered under such a working culture. In both cases, the leader is the exemplary scale

of balanced work. Finally, if the leader delegates everything but doesn't have their own non-delegated work to do, the inspiration will vanish.

A balanced investment of energy and time between hard work and rest — by both the leader and the team — brings the best sustainable example for a healthy and productive team.

HOW TO DO IT

As the highest leader, find the activities you wish to keep doing even if they could be delegated. Dedicate some hours per week to those activities. It will keep you connected with your team members on a very human and inspirational level. They will see that you are not an operations-disconnected decision-maker — instead, you will show that you can do what you ask of others and be part of the team.

And how do you keep the balance between working until exhaustion, which has nothing to do with working hard, and the excessively relaxed "feet on the table" situation? First, decide what is a good, balanced example of hard work and present it to others, not with words and theoretical explanations, but with your own behaviour and activity. Be an example. Then, constantly observe yourself and the team and to examine the situation. Be very conscious of the team dynamic. If you think that the team is falling into one of the above-described extremes, fix it. If it has to do with you, you can fix it through changing your work patterns. If it's about an individual team member, you must have a private talk and explain why this kind of work pattern is setting a bad example for others and how it can potentially harm the team and the person themselves. If it's about the group dynamic falling into one of the extremes, you can call a team meeting and go through these steps:

1. Patiently and non-personally use logic and reason to explain the current situation and what consequences it has (or may have) until everyone agrees that change is necessary.

2. Brainstorm options with the team about how the situation can be fixed.

3. In the end, come to a common solution and conclusion on which everyone agrees.

This method is extremely useful for solving any kind of individual and/or group problem.

STEPS TO TAKE

☐ Always work hard enough to be the inspiration for others and set up the standard for your team as you cannot request others to work harder than you work yourself.

☐ Delegate, but keep some activities you like to inspire yourself and others.

☐ Keep a healthy balance in your team through your own example and fix issues with the team or individuals if the balance gets broken.

PRACTICAL EXAMPLES

BUSINESS | NON-PROFITS | PRIVATE LIFE

WORK-LIFE BALANCE

Incorrect Approach

Most people in leadership positions have problems with working too much (timewise) rather than with working too little. However, this does not only apply to the leader. Everyone can get caught up in some activity to such an extent that they lose their perception of time, space and even of the people they love.

A research study showed that the second most common regret by people who are near to death is the following: "I wish I hadn't worked so hard." Do you remember that most people mistakenly exchange "working hard" with "working a lot"? Here is it the same. Therefore, allow me to adjust the statement to: "I wish I hadn't worked so much." You will never regret working hard on something that makes you happy. This is something we should always keep in our minds, as we will all be in the same situation. Here, it's extremely important to remind ourselves that our "expiration date" is written in our DNA. Therefore, it's important to make every minute, every hour, and every single day count.

Correct Approach

Here is some advice that can make you more aware of the element of time in your life and how it is spent.

My first piece of advice for you and the people you lead would be to follow Pareto's principle, which states that for approximately 80% of the effect(s) you need 20% of the cause(s). What this means is that 20% of activities are responsible for 80% of result(s). It also means that 80% activities are responsible for 20% of your desired result(s). Understanding this, make a list of all your activities. Then, carefully evaluate if they are necessary and what results they bring. This is a practical way to discard those things that consume your time and bring few or no results.

My second piece of advice is to read a good time management book or attend a good time management course. After you learn the basics, divide your life into life roles. Assign a specific colour to each of the life roles, and when you plan your calendar, you will see how much time you are spending on which life role. The first role is always "Personal" or "Me", where you plan only those things which you do by yourself. It's whatever makes you happy. The second and other roles can be, for example, wife/husband, father/mother, family, business/work, etc. Always divide the family and/or mother/father role from your husband/wife role as your relationship should always have its specific place in your calendar to keep the balance in your life. Do not create too many of them — decide which life roles are important for you and keep only those.

Many people said to me that if they start to do the things that I suggest above, they will lose their spontaneity. After they implemented these methods, they said to me that they are finally free to do what they really want and that they had mistakenly perceived chaos as spontaneity. They became fully aware of the reality of how they spend their time. This is a breathtaking experience that makes you a better and more aware leader in that you gain control over time. This is the highest level of "time leadership".

BUSINESS

WORK-LIFE BALANCE

Incorrect Approach

In business, many people think that time equals money in all situations. They say: "The longer you work, the more you'll earn." In this particular case, it's up to you what you decide. If you decide this statement is the truth, then it is the truth. If you decide it's the truth for those who think that but not for you, then you are thinking out of the box, and for you, this rule will be not valid. It's a matter of your decision.

If "time equals money in all situations" is true, we would not have examples how people got rich overnight, whether it was because they invested in the right stock or other assets at the right time or because they had an amazing idea and built up a company that brought them financial success.

Correct Approach

We all need to invest our time into work to be productive members of our society. However, if someone thinks that the more time they work, the more they will earn, and this becomes their inner system of operations, they will never come to the moment when they stop and think, "what can I do to earn more and spend less time doing it?" This brings us back to the necessity of a self-made or adopted Grand Vision which guides us through our lives and becomes the prism for our future decision-making processes at life's crossroads.

NON-PROFITS

WORK-LIFE BALANCE

Incorrect Approach

Non-profit does not mean non-work. Some people believe that they will feel good about themselves when working for a noble cause, but they aren't prepared or willing to pay the "price". In volunteer or low-paid non-profits, you always pay with your time. Don't call it a "sacrifice" as then it will become a "sacrifice". How you speak about things creates a feedback loop and determines how you will feel about them. Do not set your mind this way or your work, which should be joyful, will become bitter.

WORK-LIFE BALANCE

Correct Approach

Passion in the volunteer non-profit area comes from creating or adopting and then identifying with the Grand Vision.

Make sure that the people you lead deeply understand the cause and reason for what you do. Only then will they willingly spend their non-paid or low-paid time working with you. This is an immense responsibility as people's time is the highest value in life. They are sharing part of their life with you and each other for a Grand Vision. This example is described here from the non-profit perspective as it can show its highest standard. However, it should be copied precisely into the for-profit environment also. In addition, thankfulness and gratitude as described in the example of the previous leadership principle are especially crucial for a well-functioning non-profit team.

PRIVATE LIFE

KEEP DOING WHAT YOU LOVE

Personal Note

It's important that you do not forget yourself in between all the working and family enjoyments and obligations. There must always be room in your private life for "your own space". Your private space is where you are totally free from work or pressure from any kind of commitment in your personal or professional sphere. I will not go into detail here about what this "own space" can be. All of us have different ways of relaxing and taking care of our personal well-being. Therefore, the general advice would be to observe the occurrence of the "me colour" (= colour of your personal role as described above) in your private calendar. Make sure it appears every single week.

This is The Highest Example.

V.
Leaders must see other people on the highest level possible

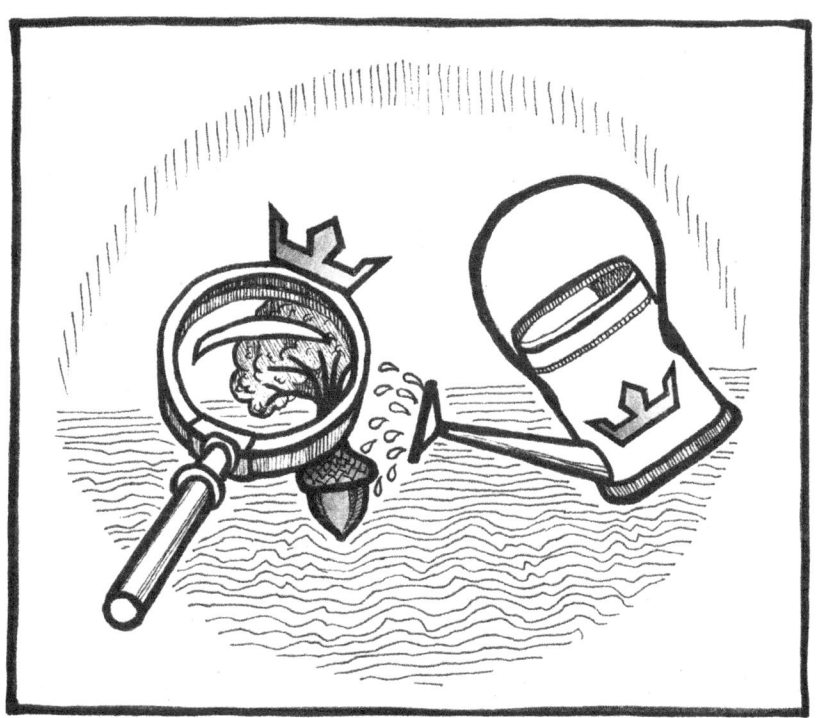

COMMON PRACTICE

It is usual for people to have functions, positions and responsibilities corresponding to their self-presentation or to their self-expectations. At the same time, leaders often focus on the mistakes of the people they lead instead of on the qualities that people have. The combination of both suppresses growth of any kind.

There is immense potential for what people can achieve. However, it can be dependent on how the leader sees them. Not everyone was born and raised with healthy self-confidence. Therefore, they do not trust their own abilities, qualities and skills. On the other hand, too much self-confidence is unhealthy and leads to careless egotism, which repels people and harms cooperation.

Generating a balanced, healthy self-confidence in team members is only the beginning of the process. Some people who have achieved healthy self-confidence are imprisoned within the limits of their own imagination and self-created inner boundaries. Many people cannot see their own potential and how much benefit they can bring to society, their families, their team members, and to themselves. Their potential is deeply frozen inside of them. To create or fulfil a Grand Vision and to feel the importance of their time invested into something meaningful is a missing element in many people's lives. Therefore, they are unhappy with the work they do.

WHY IS IT IMPORTANT?

Team members must have sufficient self-confidence; otherwise, their inner potential will stay deeply frozen and they will not be able to contribute at a high level. On the other hand, if those people who have the feeling of "I am better than others" are not corrected, their ability to be perceptive and become respected leaders themselves will be extremely limited.

When people you lead are in a balanced, self-confident state, but you do not show them the importance and meaning of their work, they will not unlock their full inner potential. This can block the great creative ideas people could have come up with and implemented.

Pulling people up builds strong personalities and admirable leaders, who will become independent and immensely thankful. Their inner potential will be unlocked, and everything becomes possible. Having such people in your team is pure joy and inspiration. Such a joyful environment also becomes contagious for all newcomers.

HOW TO DO IT

You should focus on people's qualities and imagine them in positions of great responsibility. See them on the highest level possible. If someone comes late to meetings, and at the same time is a good organizer, focus on things they do well and can develop further. It does not mean that you will excuse the fact that people behave irresponsibly. However, your main attention is on what people can achieve, not what they are doing wrong. Focus on their best abilities and quickly bring their focus to the problem so they can change their misbehaviour, but don't make this a huge deal. With that view, you will show others the highest possible example, and people will admire you for it. They will look forward to seeing you, as they know that you will show them the potential of what they can become.

Carefully assign positions, functions and responsibilities to the people with whom you work corresponding to the level on which you see them (= highest level possible), not to the level on which they currently are or to how they perceive themselves. Self-confidence, skills, and abilities will grow exponentially. People will reject too much responsibility and trust at first, but if you insist on it and reassure them, you will see the magic happen. As the leader, you must accept mistakes from the people you lead as the natural part of their development. Also, as soon as possible, switch from directive leading into delegating a whole field(s) of responsibility. Then, let people work independently on their tasks. This brings a lot of good feelings into the team.

The best way to lift people's self-confidence, if necessary, is to reassure them of their own qualities, how you see them, and remind them of the great results they've already delivered. Don't just say this once to people, but repeat it often, and people start to see themselves in the way you see them. If you see a magnificent person in front of you, and you behave accordingly towards this person, they will not be able to resist and will eventually adapt their own view about themselves to the view you have.

To correct people's overconfidence, speak with them in private about how their team members feel and how you feel when this kind of behaviour is demonstrated. You must show the person how such behaviour destroys human exchange, blocks others from opening up and makes the world seem full of uninteresting people. If you can keep an inner calm, do not hesitate to be firm and strict. People with this behavioural pattern respect even stronger behaviour than they produce themselves. You start kind but firm and end reasonable and mild.

STEPS TO TAKE

☐ Lift people's self-confidence as well as lower people's unhealthy and harmful overconfidence to achieve a balanced state. Be constantly aware, watchful, and perceptive of any sign of imbalance.

☐ "Defrost the ice" around people's potential through connecting their work with the Grand Vision. In that way, amazing and surprising qualities will be unlocked naturally.

PRACTICAL EXAMPLES

BUSINESS

PULL EVERYONE UP

Incorrect Approach

Most businesses put the newly onboarded people or current co-workers into the classic career step-by-step scheme. Their journey is designed to go from trainee through junior positions until they reach senior positions. However, this path is extremely slow, creating a gradual, linear career and personal development.

This is also why people often leave and go to different employers or business partners for better career positions and/or a wider field of responsibility. This repeats through people's whole working lives. I have had many talks with heads of HR departments and CEOs, and they say even a personnel turnover of under 10% a year costs an immense amount of time, money, and energy. To keep good workers, CEOs and HR should focus on how to show people their strengths and help to find them fields of responsibility, rather than depend on a never-ending recruitment process.

Correct Approach

I am not calling for the destruction or replacement of the necessary career and leadership structure. However, the higher you see the potential of the people you lead, the more responsibility you can assign to them. Help pull people up to positions where they do not yet see themselves. In such cases, the growth of the success of a person will be not linear, but exponential, which will be reflected in the success of your business.

Also, remember that the person who is in a trainee or junior position in your company can be assigned (or can create) a project that exceeds their job position. This is the way people grow, fully unlock their abilities and quickly progress in their development. In the beginning, this trust in them must be compensated by a higher level of supervision to prevent potential mistakes due to lack of experience. However, a lack of experience should not stop you from encouraging people to exceed the limits of their imagination and what they think and feel is possible.

NON-PROFITS

Personal Story

My non-profit experience started in the year 2014, when I had the idea of creating a global non-profit educational organization.

Immediately after having this idea, I created an empty "position mosaic" to know for whom I was looking. The key positions to fill were named "division directors", who would lead assigned global divisions. The first meeting was in the bedroom of a friend, where 10-15 people were sitting. I presented them a Grand Vision of building up a global educational organization and said that I needed people to help me. (Probably many non-profit and for-profit ideas emerged in a similar way). Some of the people said yes, some of them said no. ⟫➤

PULL EVERYONE UP

In the first few months, I positioned these amazing people as the leaders of global divisions according to the way I perceived their talents. The biggest problem was that they had not seen themselves as global division leaders. It took me more than one year before they started to feel comfortable with being called division directors. At first, when I began calling them "directors", it produced immense resistance from their side. But I never relented and always treated them as global division directors, spoke with them in that way, assigned them a global field of activity, and patiently worked with them further.

Now these people have the title "Division Director" and they are comfortable with it. We all have grown from inexperienced idealists into non-paid professionals.

PRIVATE LIFE

PULL EVERYONE UP

Personal Note

The way you see the potential of the people close to you can influence their future life as well as their self-confidence and self-perception. Your view and the way you express it can lift up people you care about as well as put them down hard. This is true especially within the family and in relationships, where there is a high level of interpersonal openness. This emotional openness enables you to help those whom you love to see themselves on the level you see them — on the highest level possible. You can help them to create their own vision, show them their possibilities and their personal value as well. Seeing as many people as possible on the highest level possible and sharing this view with them will become an integral part of your functioning. This is the highest view you can maintain all the time. However, judge wisely when to share your view. In time, you will master the understanding of the right time and the right moment.

This is The Highest Example.

VI.
Leaders must see themselves on the highest level possible

COMMON PRACTICE

We have learned how to see others on the highest level possible, and now the next challenge is to see ourselves in the same way. Many leaders are not always successful at balancing between the two extremes. First is the "I am better than the others" state, which makes them ultimately alone as it repulses the people they lead. Secondly, there is the "Everyone is better than me" and/or "I can't handle it" state of mind, which is not normally expressed in words, but it is felt by everyone around and results in the loss of trust in the leader.

The next mistake is that leaders are often confused about where they stand in relation towards the people they lead. Are they above the people they lead or equal with them? The answer is — both. It is true that the leader of a group of people is structurally and hierarchically above the others. That's the practical and logical level; both you and the people you lead should be very clear about this, especially in times of crisis, when the team must function as one body, one mind, one machine, one powerful factory. The ideas above are achieved through crystal-clear awareness of who is the leader and who is being led.

However, on the level of how one perceives people, the leader should see them as equal in their personal value. Many leaders have a problem with clearly understanding the meaning of "above" and/or "equal" in relation to their function. They lead people either like bunch of friends on a spring break and behave accordingly, or as merciless autocrats. Leaders often think it's one or the other, but balance is the answer.

WHY IS IT IMPORTANT?

Once you doubt yourself, the people you lead start to doubt you too. If you behave like an alpha-leader, people will close themselves off from you. If you behave like friend from high school, people will lose respect for you, and this is very hard to build up again.

Having healthy self-confidence and being able to feel equal to others while not forgetting your leadership position will gain you a lot of openness from people you lead. They will perceive you as someone to whom they can be honest, and they will feel deep respect.

HOW TO DO IT

This is the way to act:

☐ You are the leader. This must be clear to all the people you lead and, most importantly, to yourself. In the areas of structure, hierarchy and representation of the Grand Vision, you are the one in charge. This in indisputable and undeniable. Therefore, you must behave accordingly. You carry the final and ultimate responsibility for the results and for every single mistake of each team member you lead. When necessary, you must act as the protector and even use reasoned directive (= explaining why) as the tool for preventing any kind of potentially troubling situation.

When there is no crisis, which is the normal situation, you give the space for people to work on their own, supporting and guiding them and expressing full trust in them. If interference is necessary, you can switch to the solution described in the paragraph above. The leader must master the ability of skilfully moving between these two methods of leadership through their own experience.

If friendship naturally develops with some of the people you lead, you have to be sure that it's with those you trust 100%, who will not misuse the new relationship. At the same time, no one in your team should be treated better than the others. Regardless of whether it is your husband, wife, friend or family member that is in your team, you have to treat them exactly as you would treat anyone else. There should be no special treatment for anyone.

This is the way to think:

☐ How you see yourself and the people you lead matters immensely. People can feel how you see them and how you see yourself without any words being said. Therefore, you must see yourself as the leader and be aware of your position and responsibility. At the same time, you see others as equal to you with no exception. Do not confuse equality with seeing all others as "the same" since everyone is different and has different qualities. You must learn how to see people as equal to you, and at the same time, be able to lead them in the two modes described above. Most of the time you give them space to do their job, but, if necessary, you might have to interfere and lead in a directive way. Both modes are completely okay as long as you keep the feeling of appreciation, thankfulness and equality inside of you towards the people you lead.

If you ever doubt your own abilities, understand that this happens to many leaders from time to time. If you are in such a state of mind, it is good to remind yourself about what you have already achieved in your life. If you have trouble doing this exercise, find someone who likes you, knows you, and can help you to see what you can't. However, the most important thing is to never give in to that state of mind. Feelings like this will come and go all your life, and the more you focus on them, the more they will hinder your performance. Let them go and be the highest example for others. This is a prime responsibility for all of us.

STEPS TO TAKE

☐ Lead through balance, give space as well as firm directions, but keep the feeling of equality between you and the people you lead.

☐ Let go of your doubts about your abilities. If you find this hard to do, ask a close friend for help.

☐ No special treatment for anyone.

PRACTICAL EXAMPLES

BUSINESS  | NON-PROFITS

THE FUTURE IS NOW

Incorrect Approach

Many leaders were taught in school to adopt the idea of gradual personal development. This is the idea of gradually becoming successful. It goes hand in hand with the self-perception of the leader. The higher your see yourself, the higher you will be seen by others, regardless of current conditions. The Grand Vision is what you present to others. Identification with the current state and situation keeps others from seeing the excellence of the leader's qualities. I've met many people who had amazing ideas, even a great vision, but instead of identifying with their future vision, they identified themselves with their current state. Self-perception decides everything.

Correct Approach

We previously covered the principle that a business is built up from the Grand Vision which flows top-down and not bottom-up. We understand that it is necessary to see people on the highest level possible, so that they will grow exponentially and, sooner rather than later, become what you see in them. Now is the time to decide that you are what you want to be and not where you currently are. If you have a small team, but Grand Vision, you must identify with the Grand Vision. This is where you belong mentally. In such a way, all doors and all hearts are open. Identify with your Grand Vision, not with your current bank account balance.

JOB INTERVIEW(S)

If you are the one going to the job interview, this is precisely the point where the future must become the present.

In this moment, you decide if you will present only your current experience and skills, or if you will properly prepare and visualize everything that could be accomplished through your participation in the company. If the company has a vision, study it and find out how you can, through the offered position, be part of its realization. This is immensely attractive to the one who is interviewing you, especially if you have the possibility to speak directly with the owner or CEO. With this approach, you strongly increase the chance of being chosen and can even ask for more money. Of course, you have to be prepared to commit totally to the job and fulfil the expectations you've created.

If you are the one who is conducting the job interview, this is exactly the point where the future must become the present.

In this moment, you must decide if you will present to the applicant the current stage of development of your company or if you will properly prepare yourself and visualize everything that can be accomplished through their participation in your company. Use the vision of the company and find out how, through the offered position, the applicant can be part of its realization. This is attractive to the one who is being interviewed. With this approach, you will have a better chance that the person will choose to work with you. There will be also a better chance that they will accept a lower salary in exchange for being part of your vision. Of course, you must be prepared to fulfil the expectations you've created.

BUSINESS

THE FUTURE IS NOW

Additional Note

I have been a witness to too many cases when great companies felt they "were not big enough", "not professional enough", "not competitive enough" or "not experienced enough". This mental self-limitation stopped them from thinking big and going beyond the status quo. You must make sure that the company you own or work for is self-confident enough in its public presentation, as well in its internal self-presentation. All people who represent the company to the outside world must feel, regardless of the size and experience of the company, that you aim for the "Olympics", not the "village match".

It is not about the competition, it is about having a Grand Vision and going for it. Many people may not feel confident enough because of the size of their company. However, "small company" is a very subjective term; one person may perceive a company with 10 employees as small, while someone who makes deals with huge enterprises with thousands of employees may perceive a company with 100,000 employees as small. The greatness of the company is defined by its Grand Vision, not by its current size or turnover. The leader must make people understand, see, and feel the vision inside and out, and everything will naturally grow.

NON-PROFITS

THE FUTURE IS NOW

Personal Story

I remember when I printed my first business cards in a newly established NGO. My title on the cards was "Vice-President & CEO" even though there were 10 people in the team. We had no office, and no public recognition. However, in every single communication with high officials, when I asked for an appointment, I behaved, dressed, and communicated like a Vice-President & CEO of a global educational organization. I couldn't say that we had already achieved a global scale of activity, but I could always share the Grand Vision, representing the direction we were going. ⟫

>> People immediately identified us as those who would achieve great progress in the future. Therefore, they took us seriously in the present. Identification with the visualized future is the most important principle for gaining acceptance and recognition, regardless of where you are in the process right now. This is what I teach all new team members, as well as encouraging them to teach their team members and so on.

PRIVATE LIFE

THE FUTURE IS NOW

Personal Note

If the people around you already see their potential and have started to see themselves as you see them — on the highest level possible — then the next natural step is to show them how to keep this healthy view of themselves without your assistance. To teach your close ones to identify with their vision and not their current state is of great importance. In that way, they can gain strength, increase their self-confidence and recognize their self-value. It will help them tremendously in all situations in their lives.

They should have balanced self-confidence, self-perception and identify with the visualized future without the necessity of any word being spoken. Their body posture, facial expression as well as the sound of their voice will change. Every move, look and verbal exchange will attest the stability and power of the vision.

This is The Highest Example.

VII.
Leaders must take over responsibility immediately

COMMON PRACTICE

Many leaders tend to take over the responsibility of leadership in slow-motion. It's often connected with an inner or, even worse, publicly expressed reasoning that "First, I need to know how things function here, before I take over" or "First, I will get to know all of you and then I will take over" or "First, I will master one leadership principle, before I start to follow the next one" and so on. This slow way of taking over responsibility is unhealthy for the team spirit and the position of the leader as such. In minor cases, it's connected with a lack of the leader's self-confidence, but most of the time it's connected with the way we were taught by a variety of people during our lives. We were told that the correct way to function is gradually, step-by-step. Our whole society is based on gradual step-by-step processes, with little possibility to skip a class in school, a job position in the company or a level in any kind of certification process. However, this is a weakness in leadership.

WHY IS IT IMPORTANT?

The gradual "slow-motion" takeover of responsibility will be considered as a sign of the leader's weakness. The people you lead will forgive the mistakes you make if you are 100% invested in the process. However, they will not forgive you a cautious "I want to play it safe" approach towards yourself, your work and towards them.

Immediately taking responsibility is considered the sign of a leader's strength. In this scenario, you may make mistakes because of what you do and say, but you are active, not passive. Your courage will cause people to feel your authority, and they will give 100% to you from day one.

HOW TO DO IT

People do not become leaders. People decide to be leaders. Being a leader is an inner decision made in a moment, and not a gradual thought process. Once you decide to be the leader, you are the leader. There are many great stories from history when a young king or queen took over leadership of their country, as was customary in those times, since their predecessors died prematurely. The young leaders had to identify with their newly acquired position and responsibility. With the support of experienced advi-

sors, they had to take over immediately. They didn't agree to be in charge and often had no preparation period.

You should think about being a leader in a similar way. You have decided to take the responsibility, therefore you "own" it. The people you lead expect strength, support, healthy self-confidence and a show of immediate power to make decisions. The truth is that no one is interested in how much you still have to learn and how much you still don't know. The important point is this: people want a leader who will lead them toward the Grand Vision and take responsibility for it.

You cannot try the decision before you make it. You are the leader from the day one. You follow all the leadership principles from the very beginning and you become the iron spine of the team you lead. It is the well-being of the others that is at stake.

STEPS TO TAKE

☐ Being the leader is the matter of an inner decision and identification with the highest principles.

☐ Leading others is a matter of immediately taking over responsibility, regardless of any possible mistakes made during the process.

PRACTICAL EXAMPLES

BUSINESS  | NON-PROFITS

100% LEADER FROM DAY ONE

Incorrect Approach

Slow or insecure takeover of any kind of responsibility creates negative perceptions about the leader and has conscious and subconscious effects on the people witnessing it. If the person taking responsibility grows gradually through a variety of positions and is known by the teams, this situation may not happen. Or there may be no negative perception when the type of the work does not change in any unpredictable way. However, when you are assigned to a completely new team, replacing another leader for whatever reason, or taking over a totally different type of work than you are used to, then the natural tendency is to "play it safe" as described above. I've seen too many great leaders who started to feel insecure because of such conditions.

Correct Approach

A quick and confident takeover of any kind of responsibility creates positive perceptions about the leader and has conscious and subconscious effects on the people who witness it.

If you are assigned to a team you haven't worked with before or meet for the first time, it's very important to show which areas you are strong in and do what people will not expect. Instead of starting with numbers and charts, organize a seminar or workshop on the leadership principles mentioned in this book for your whole team, so that you can teach people how you work yourself and why, and what you expect from others and why. Regardless of your field of expertise, you are the leader, and you are working with people. Therefore, you must be the master of leadership — you are the highest example. Your leadership skills are something you can always rely on and share with others. ≫→

100% LEADER FROM DAY ONE

Don't be the "all-knowing" leader. Make your team your advisors. People will see that you consider their input and ideas, but also, they should see that you will make the final decision. In the end, you are the only one who will carry the responsibility for the decisions being made.

Leading people is an art and a craft. It's certainly not a soft skill that you can learn in the same way as presentation techniques or project planning. Therefore, the principles mentioned in this book can be a legacy that you can pass on to others. In this way, you can shine from day one, regardless of the business or volunteer area in which you are engaged.

BUSINESS | NON-PROFITS | PRIVATE LIFE

CRISIS LEADERSHIP

Personal Note

The highest leadership is to take over immediately. A positive side-effect of immediate responsibility takeover is that the leader is perceived as self-confident and strong, like an iron pier in the middle of a sea storm. It is immensely important to boldly, correctly and non-emotionally identify the situation and take over the responsibility for solving it immediately, especially if you are handling complicated life situations like health problems, legal difficulties or any other business, personal or family crisis. The tougher the crisis, the stronger the leader must be. If we see that we can help to solve the problem, we must do it as soon as possible. Regardless of the kind of decisions being made, a transfer of responsibility naturally comes with them. The quicker the problem is solved, the faster the pain or discomfort disappears. You should always go sleep with the feeling that you gave your best and did everything you could.

This is The Highest Example.

VIII.
Leaders are firm when cooperation begins

COMMON PRACTICE

Many leaders, when they begin cooperating with a new person, tend use a mild, gentle manner of communication. The first moments of a first encounter are decisive for setting up the standard of the future cooperation and exchange between the leader and the team member. Being too mild causes people to lose respect towards the leader.

The leader will need, from time to time, to be extremely firm and clear. If people don't experience this aspect of leadership from the beginning, they will tend go against the leader and could be resistant, causing disruption in the team. Once the leader has shown power, firmness, and clarity in the first moments of the first meeting, then the people will accept similar behaviour in the future. However, resistance and disruptions of the team members can be also caused by a leader's misbehaviour. Therefore, precaution, maturity and self-reflection are especially important for following this specific leadership principle.

If this principle is not observed, the next consequence is that leaders start to be afraid of those they lead, fearing that, in certain situations, people could react unexpectedly and potentially leave the team or quit cooperating.

WHY IS IT IMPORTANT?

When you are not clear and firm at the beginning of the cooperation, people will not store this impression of your behaviour in their memory. Then, when there's a time where you need to behave firmly, there will be nothing they can refer to, and you can expect resistance, disrespect and confrontation.

If you are clear and firm at the beginning, people will store this impression of you inside of them. When you need to behave firmly, they will invoke this memory and not resist irrationally.

HOW TO DO IT

Everything starts with the first encounter. Once there is a relationship between the leader and team member who follows, the countdown for the leader to show firmness and clarity starts.

The best way for the leader to implement this principle is to share all the information that can potentially create any kind of disagreement or conflict with the team members. Of course, this should be done after sharing the Grand Vision. Everything has its pros and cons. Present both, but do not avoid the cons. Present them firmly and wait for people's responses. If there is resistance, go into the reasons for the activity or rule, and have a calm debate.

Show immediately at the beginning of the cooperation that people can come to you with any concern they may have. Listen to everyone's worries and then have a firm but fair debate. When you know you are right according to the principles, debate until you clarify your argument. In situations where you are not sure, let the debate decide what action or decision will be followed. This kind of approach gives people the feeling that they can come to you anytime for a discussion. However, they also should know they will need to defend every single suggestion, point or idea that they would like to have accepted.

The idea is to always present both sides of the issue, not only one side. The firmer and clearer you are, the more it will attract like-minded people and repel people you don't want to work with anyway. This makes for a great filter and saves you time and energy in the future.

If you already lead a team and you haven't followed this principle or you are afraid to speak in a firm way about various issues with the people you lead, introduce the concept of each new idea always being debated and that you will be part of the debate. If some rules are broken and principles are not followed, bring the issue to the whole team and create a public debate. If you are sure that you are right and that the truth is on your side, you will be the winner of the debate and people will have this memory of your fearless and clear behaviour in a potentially troublesome and uneasy situation. Their memory of this situation will help you in the future.

STEPS TO TAKE

☐ In the first moments of any cooperation, share the Grand Vision with people and immediately follow up with all potentially controversial topics connected with the work they will do. Debate, if necessary, until everyone is clear and there are no unresolved issues. In this way, you will show your fearlessness when going into difficult situations.

☐ Do not be afraid to speak about anything with the people you lead. Do not have any fear that people will leave if you are firm. Do not fear handling difficult situations. Solve issues through debate.

PRACTICAL EXAMPLES

BUSINESS  | NON-PROFITS

CREATE BOUNDARIES

Incorrect Approach	Many leaders avoid public debate within their teams because it is unpleasant. They feel and know the exact moments when a difficult topic must be publicly or individually raised, but do not engage it. These are situations which shape team spirit, clarity, and integrity. When they are not addressed because of whatever reason (being afraid, unpleasant feelings, not enough confidence, etc.), it creates an example for all other future situations. The more unsolved difficult situations accumulate, the more work, time and energy it will cost and the more unpleasant the situation will become in the end. Being afraid to open the wounds does not solve anything. As a small amount of painful disinfectant is better than a life-threatening inflammation, prevention is better than repression. Unwillingness to go into an unpleasant situation will only make things worse.
Correct Approach	Always look for unsolved troubles and problems and open them up to discussion immediately. Sort them out now, today or tomorrow. But do not postpone action. The more you postpone a collective or individual search for the solution of the problem, the more it will hurt everyone later. It is the job of the leader to be firm and clear in debating internal as well as external issues. Adopt a crystal-clear, fearless approach, cut into the unhealthy wounds, and let them disinfect and heal through mature debate. If you see any breach of rules and principles, do what is right, not what feels good. There are situations, especially if you are attacked from the outside, when it's better to maintain strategic silence. However, internal team issues must be tackled immediately, and people should be always be encouraged to share their problems with you as soon as they sense them.

CREATE BOUNDARIES

**Personal
Story**

In non-profit, non-paid work, this principle is the alpha and omega of all the cooperation between the leader and others, as people do not expect firm behaviour when applying to become volunteers. When I onboard new people into the team, I always start by seeking an agreement from both sides that there is a problem to be solved. When there is an agreement, I continue to present the Grand Vision which solves the problem and, immediately afterwards, I share all the rules and obligations. This is the best that you can do as the person who is right for the team may debate with you a bit, but finally will accept your terms and conditions and join the team.

Most of the time, the unsuitability of a person who wouldn't fit in the team becomes apparent during the first interview. If you don't follow these steps during the first interview — where the person should be presented with all the "terms and conditions" — and they are then accepted onto the team, it can create immensely unpleasant conversations later on. Even worse, it can lead to strong public disagreements, setting a bad example for the other team members witnessing it. Be honest and do not step aside. Stay firm in what you say and make no exceptions. You need people to follow all internal rules, principles, and obligations 100%. Once you make one exception, you will always make others.

VIII. Leaders are firm when cooperation begins

PRIVATE LIFE

CREATE BOUNDARIES

Personal Note

In every relationship, business or private, it is good to set boundaries. In the business environment, the boundaries are codified within contracts and agreements, usually in the written form. Business agreements state what is expected and allowed, or not allowed, and in every deal a participant knows, agrees to, and finally consents to the content with their signature.

This is not how it works within the family, between friends, or in relationships. However, those close to us have their own inner expectations regarding what they do and do not like. One of the healthiest things that can happen to us and those we care for is a verbal exchange of our expectations as soon as possible. Here, I am not speaking about which ice cream your life partner likes, but rather about their (and your) ideas, vision, and views on relationships.

In many countries, the divorce rate is near 50% (and the rate of separation of non-married couples would make this number even higher). Every divorce or end of long-term relationship is accompanied by a great deal of emotional, financial, family, and legal trouble. Therefore, an honest talk with your future wife/husband/potential life partner is for the good of all. If you understand each other, there is no guessing or making things up, which can lead to hurt feelings and misunderstandings. This can bring a lot of happiness into the life of both and to the whole family. Having this kind of honest exchange does not guarantee a life-long relationship, but you will know that you did your best.

This is The Highest Example.

IX.
Leaders explain the reasons for their requests

COMMON PRACTICE

People work for many different reasons. For example, people work because it is expected by their family, partner, society or it is requested by the leader of their team. They execute their tasks and projects even if they don't understand its importance for themselves, their company and others. This means people often dislike what they do. Not because they really don't enjoy their work, but because they perceive it as meaningless. This can lead to the feeling of dissatisfaction or even to a general loss of interest. This feeling of insignificance and futility of their personal input is followed by a loss of inner motivation.

There are no insignificant jobs, businesses or activities, nor are there any senseless rules, principles and laws as long as they are logically reasoned. Behind every request and regulation, there should be some deeper understanding connected with a positive or negative experience. Then, those who should follow these rules would understand their meaning totally. However, most of the time, leaders do not transfer their understanding and experience to the person. They delegate the field of responsibility, ask others to do a task or to follow a procedure.

WHY IS IT IMPORTANT?

Not communicating requests in the proper way lowers quality. If people do not really understand why they do certain things, they do not care as much as they would if they knew the reasons.

Communicating requests in the proper way increases loyalty and productivity. When people have understanding, they will do things even when no one is watching. They will work with passion, enthusiasm and dedication.

HOW TO DO IT

This principle is one of the easiest to follow. There is a simple way to change your communication with the people you lead, individually or collectively, so that the inner feeling of "I am obliged to do what I am requested to" transforms into "I deeply understand the meaning of what I am requested to do, so I want to do it." You can achieve the "I want to do it" attitude of the people you lead by explaining why they should do what they are asked.

If you ask people to do something, they should understand how the requested activity relates to the fulfilment of the vision. This can be people's jobs, projects, events, etc.

If you wish for people to follow your leadership, they must understand the experience which led to the creation of a new rule or regulation. In these cases, you point out what negative consequences you want to avoid and what positive consequences you want to achieve by using the rule. In this way, people understand and follow the rules willingly.

Every single request you make, verbal or written, should be underlined with an explanation of why you want others to follow, process or execute it. Every single internal policy and rule should be explained in detail. If logic, common sense, and kindness are applied, the majority of the people you lead will always understand it.

You should always keep your door open for people who need an extended explanation. Doing this, you will make sure that every single request will be followed due to their understanding and willingness instead of obligation.

It is immensely important that this principle is reflected in all of your communications. Remember that there is no insignificant e-mail, chat message, SMS, social media post, speech, one-to-one talk, exchange, interview, invitation to any kind of event, etc.

This whole book was written in exactly the way that is described above: Every chapter has its repetitive explanatory, experience-based structure, which describes the importance of each principle in multiple ways, so the meaning is fully transferred to all readers, regardless of their different personality types. These different explanatory views will help you when teaching others. Three ways of explaining are always better than one. Therefore, you have three different types of reasoning in this book:

1. Every principle is explained through logic
   ("Common Practice" and "How to do it" Section)

2. Every principle is explained through feeling
   ("Why is it important?" Section)

3. Every principle is explained through experience
   ("Practical Examples" Section)

All three types of reasoning are supported by an artistic expression through illustrations and symbols.

STEPS TO TAKE

☐ Make sure that the people you lead always execute your requests and follow all regulations because they deeply understand why they are important.

☐ Through patient explanation of every single request or regulation, you make sure that the people you lead will start to adopt the "I want to" attitude, instead of "I have to" attitude.

☐ Use multiple ways of reasoning — based on logic, feeling and experience — and, if you can, support them with simple, memorable symbols and graphics. If you use only one way, it's better than none. If you use two ways, then it's good. If you use all three ways, this is the highest example.

PRACTICAL EXAMPLES

BUSINESS | NON-PROFITS

COMMUNICATION

| **Incorrect Approach** | It has happened to all of us, as leaders or team members, that at some point we had to follow and/or we asked others to follow a poorly reasoned request. Many times, the reason for there being no explanation was that the person requesting it thought it was so obvious that no explanation was needed. Or it could be caused by someone thinking that they were the authority and, therefore, didn't need to give any explanation. In most cases, we did what we had to do, or other people did what we requested, but it does not make us great leaders. This is not the long-term way to show the highest example. |
| **Correct Approach** | Of course, you can and should make requests from the position of your authority, but if you want to be the highest example of leadership, then this is not enough. If you want things to be done from general willingness and not obligation, people need to understand the meaning of your request. ⤻ |

» This attitude must be reflected even at the micro-level. When you call people to an extra meeting, give a reason why. When you introduce new rule, give a reason why. When you invite everyone to an annual conference, give reasons why. Make reasoning an integral part of your communication, both internal and external.

BUSINESS

Additional Note

In the for-profit area, you have the mighty element of money playing in your favour. So, even if you do not follow this principle, you may get things done anyway. However, if you want people to believe deeply in your cause, to make them comfortable and self-assured in explaining your requests to others, and to perceive you as their leader and example, then you need to implement this principle of reasoning within your company or team. You will stop having employees and co-workers, and instead will produce new leaders who will follow you and on whom you can rely. This is one of the strongest connections you can aim for.

NON-PROFITS

Additional Note

In the non-profit and especially in the volunteer arena, this is the only way to build up a great team of amazing people who do everything out of their inner understanding of the Grand Vision and these leadership principles. With the non-profit, you don't have another option. If you do not implement and adapt your communication according to this principle, you will never build up successful team of strong leaders following you anytime, anywhere.

PRIVATE LIFE

COMMUNICATION

Personal Note

Many personal conflicts would be avoided if those close to you knew why you do the things you decide to do.

If you start to work on a noble cause, make sure that you gain the support of your loved ones first. This is especially true if you plan on dedicating a significant amount of your free time to any volunteer activity that will reduce your availability to your family and friends. If they deeply understand your reasons, you will gain not only acceptance, but also extraordinarily strong support. However, do not forget the work-life balance and wise distribution of your time as described in the previous leadership principles. Do not take the support from your loved ones for granted and include them into your world of ideas.

This is The Highest Example.

X.
Leaders create balance

COMMON PRACTICE

Leaders must find and keep the balance between:

☐ **Freedom and order.** Leaders must watch out for falling into extremes. Many leaders give too much freedom and lose healthy control over their team members. Others enforce order so harshly that people run from them and do not want to work with them, regardless of the greatness of their vision.

☐ **Kindness and firmness.** Leaders must avoid inappropriate reactions in different situations. If people need support, openness and a big heart, and instead they receive iron-like strictness, they will see the leader as inhuman, cold and distant. If people need to be reminded of clear rules, principles and structure, and their leader delivers kindness, gentleness and even sentimentality, they will see the leader as weak, soft and incapable of action. Being able to manoeuvre between these two types of behaviour is not something you can learn from theory; it is a principle that you "learn by doing". However, all leaders need to know this principle and become conscious of it.

☐ **Excitation and calmness.** Leaders must prevent hyped-up or boring environments. Leaders should keep excitement long enough for people to feel inspiration and stay calm long enough for people to feel relaxed.

WHY IS IT IMPORTANT?

When the principle of balance is not taken into consideration, people will feel that you are unstable and unpredictable. You have to always strive for iron-like stability and emotional predictability. The feeling of instability is contagious, causing others to behave unpredictably, too. This can cause a variety of problems for the whole group.

When you have achieved a balance, you can consciously decide how to react correctly in a variety of situations and circumstances. Later your reactions will be so automatic that you will run on "auto-pilot". Being able to predict the leader's reactions is very healthy for people as they need to feel stability from the person they follow.

HOW TO DO IT

You must always be aware of how people are feeling under your leadership. People will accept both sides (freedom and order, kindness and firmness, excitation and calmness) if delivered appropriately to the situation. People will generally accept firm or gentle behaviour when it is non-personal, properly reasoned, and fitting to the circumstance. Observe not only your behaviour, but also people's reactions to your behaviour, how they feel about what, and especially how you express yourself.

To makes things even easier and quicker to learn, there is a possible accelerator: there are two main types of personalities. One type mainly decides and acts from logic. The second type mainly decides and acts from feelings. Both of these responses are legitimate and natural. The first type will have more trouble with being too firm, and the second type will have trouble with being too kind.

First, identify which type you are. Second, find a person in your team who can give you feedback. If you have a more logical personality, find a mature and emotionally receptive person. If you have a more feelings-based personality, find a mature and logically reasoning person. This will become your private feedback mechanism. Choose this person wisely. It must be someone you totally trust and who will never share your talks with anyone else in your team. Ask this person to give you feedback before or after each of your spoken or written communications with your team members. If you are in the middle, between the logical and feeling-based personality, find two advisors, one who is logical and the other feeling-based.

STEPS TO TAKE

☐ Become aware of your day-to-day behaviour and how it's perceived by your team. Observe the internal dynamics and the overall feeling within your team.

☐ If necessary, find a personal advisor in the team — one who has a personality opposite to yours and is mature and trustworthy — to give you honest feedback.

☐ Find the balance through your own experience by trial and error.

PRACTICAL EXAMPLES

BUSINESS | NON-PROFITS | PRIVATE LIFE

QUOTATIONS

I've learned much from the book *The Art of War*, written approximately 2,500 years ago by Sun Tzu, one of the most famous military strategists of all time. *The Art of War* is a highly practical work, used not only in strategic military education, but also as an up-to-date guide for for-profit & non-profit endeavours, and even for use in people's private lives.

Sun Tzu summarized the importance of balance between firmness and kindness, freedom and order. This principle is one of the hardest to absorb since it's not only about your decision to follow it, but also because it is only through trial and error that you can gain the experience needed to apply it properly. It is the principle where most leaders make mistakes. Therefore, please read the following lines with your full attention.

Quotes retrieved from:
Sun Tzŭ
ON THE
ART OF WAR
THE OLDEST MILITARY TREATISE IN THE WORLD

Translated from the Chinese by LIONEL GILES, M.A.
(London, LUZAC & Co., 1910)

• • •

"Therefore soldiers must be treated in the first instance with humanity, but kept under control by means of iron discipline. This is a certain road to victory."
p. 98, Chapter IX., Section 43

"If in training soldiers commands are habitually enforced, the army will be well-disciplined; if not, its discipline will be bad."
p. 98 Chapter IX., Section 44

"If a general shows confidence in his men but always insists on his orders being obeyed, the gain will be mutual."
p.98-99, Chapter IX., Section 45

"When the common soldiers are too strong and their officers too weak, the result is insubordination. When the officers are too strong and the common soldiers too weak, the result is collapse."
p. 105-106, Chapter X., Section 16

"If, however, you are indulgent, but unable to make your authority felt; kind-hearted, but unable to enforce your commands; and incapable, moreover, of quelling disorder: then your soldiers must be likened to spoilt children; they are useless for any practical purpose."
p. 111, Chapter X., Section 26

This is The Highest Example.

Milan provides Individual & Group Consultancy Services.

For more information and appointments, go to:

www.Podlipny.info

Made in the USA
Monee, IL
07 July 2026

56552347R00046